How do I say that?

Written by **Sue Wise**
Illustrated by **Christine Coirault**

Editor: Annabel Blackledge
Editorial Director: Louise Pritchard
Design Director: Jill Plank

Pangolin Books and Sue Wise would like to thank Virginie Mondon, French
assistant at Pate's Grammar School, Cheltenham, for her help with the text.

First published in the UK in 2005 by Pangolin Books
Unit 17, Piccadilly Mill, Lower Street, Stroud, Gloucestershire, GL5 2HT

A CIP catalogue record for this book is available from the British Library.

ISBN 1-84493-022-X

Colour reproduction by Black Cat Graphics Ltd, Bristol, UK
Printed in China by Compass Press Ltd

Contents

The French language

There are a few things you should know about the French language before you try to speak it. Take a few minutes to read the information below, and you will enjoy this book all the more.

Masculine, feminine, plural

All French nouns are either masculine or feminine. If a word has *le* (the), *un* (a), *ce* (this), *mon* (my) or *ton* (your) in front of it, it is masculine. And if a word has *la* (the), *une* (a), *cette* (this), *ma* (my) or *ta* (your) in front of it, it is feminine. Plural nouns, both masculine and feminine, have *les* (the), *ces* (these), *des* (some), *mes* (my) or *tes* (your) in front of them. If a noun begins with a vowel, *le* and *la* are shortened to *l'*, as in *l'école* (the school). Some adjectives have an 'e' on the end if the noun they are describing is feminine, but no 'e' if the noun is masculine, as in *petite/petit* (small). Adjectives have an 's' or an 'x' on the end if the noun is plural.

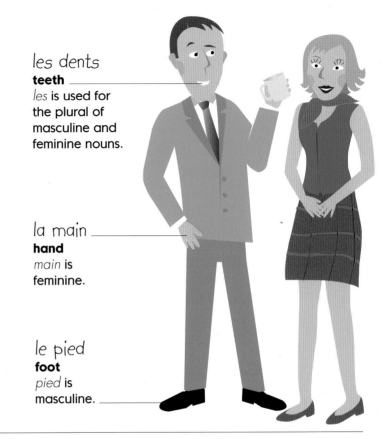

les dents
teeth
les is used for the plural of masculine and feminine nouns.

la main
hand
main is feminine.

le pied
foot
pied is masculine.

How verbs change

French verbs change according to the subject of the sentence (the person who is doing the action). Some verbs follow regular patterns, but others do not. Here are examples of how three different French verbs change. You will find that the verbs *être* and *avoir* are used often in French. These lists will help you recognize them in this book.

manger – to eat
(a regular verb)
je mange (**I eat**)
tu manges (**you eat**)
il/elle mange (**he/she eats**)
nous mangeons (**we eat**)
vous mangez (**you eat**)
ils/elles mangent (**they eat**)

être – to be
(an irregular verb)
je suis (**I am**)
tu es (**you are**)
il/elle est (**he/she is**)
nous sommes (**we are**)
vous êtes (**you are**)
ils/elles sont (**they are**)

avoir – to have
(an irregular verb)
j'ai (**I have**)
tu as (**you have**)
il/elle a (**he/she has**)
nous avons (**we have**)
vous avez (**you have**)
ils/elles ont (**they have**)

Saying it in French

- Read the pronunciation guides beneath the French as if they were English.

- Some French words run together when they are spoken. The guides show these as one word.
- In French, all the syllables in a word have equal stress on them, unlike English words.
- The French 'r' sound is said in the back of the throat – lots of saliva needed!
- Lots of French words have silent letters at the end. For example, *gâteaux* (cake) sounds like 'gattoh' and *les œufs* (eggs) sounds like 'layzeur' and the 'n' at the end of *mon* (my) is usually silent.
- The French words *a* (has) and *à* (to/at) sound like the 'a' at the start of the English word apple.

- Pronounce 'uh', as in 'suh' – *ce* (this), 'puh' – *peut* (can) and 'kuh' – *que* (that), like the 'a' in the English word along.
- 'Jh', as in 'jhombon'– *jambon* (ham), is a soft sound, like the 'g' in the English word mirage.
- Say 'eur', as in 'beur' – *beurre* (butter), like 'urr' in the English word purr, but a bit longer and more drawn out.
- Say 'yur', as in 'confityur' – *confiture* (jam), like the 'ure' in the English word pure, but emphasise the 'y' sound.
- In 'ang', as in 'pang' – *pain* (bread), the 'g' is soft and nasal. Try holding your nose when you say it!

Bien, allons-y.
Beeang, allonzee.
OK, let's get started.

Napoléon's thoughts

Napoléon the dog always has something amusing on his mind. When you see a thought bubble in French, try to guess what Napoléon is saying to himself.

Then turn to page 32 to find out if you are right. Different countries have different sayings, so you may be surprised when you discover exactly what Napoléon is thinking!

la confiture
la confityur
jam

Papa
Pappa
Dad

la tasse
la tass
cup

Maman
Mammon
Mum

la cuisinière
la kweezeenyair
cooker

le café
luh kafay
coffee

la cuillère
la kweeyair
spoon

le jus d'orange
luh jhew doronjh
orange juice

le couteau
luh kootoh
knife

la chaise
la shairz
chair

la mallette
la malett
briefcase

Peux-tu nettoyer mon **couteau**, Papa? Il est tombé par terre.
Puh tew netwayay mon kootoh, Pappa? Eel ay tombay par tair.
Can you clean my knife, Dad? It has fallen on the floor.

Éteinds la **cuisinière**! Le repas va brûler!
Aytang la kweezeenyair. Luh repa va brewlay!
Turn off the cooker! The food will burn!

Le pain goûte bien meilleur avec le **beurre**.
Luh pang goote beeang mayeur avek luh beur.
Bread tastes much better with some butter.

Papa adore la **confiture** de fraise.
Pappa adoor la confityur duh fraiz.
Dad adores strawberry jam.

J'ai laissé mes livres d'école sur la **chaise** – ne vous asseyez pas dessus!
Jhay lessay may leevr daycoll syur la shairz – nuh voozassayay pa dessew!
I left my school books on the chair – don't sit on them!

Maman dit que le **lait** est merveilleux pour les os.
Mammon dee kuh luh lay ay mairvayer poor layzoh.
Mum says that milk is brilliant for your bones.

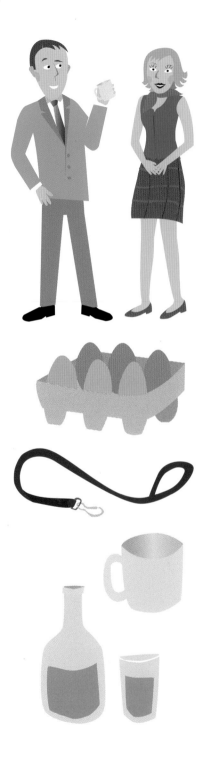

Maman fait mon petit déjeuner tous les matins – elle est très gentille.

Mammon fay mon petee dayjheurnay too lay mattang – ell ay tray jhonteey.

Mum makes my breakfast every morning – she is very kind.

Papa est toujours en retard au travail.

Pappa ay toojhoor on retar oh trav-eye.

Dad is always late for work.

J'aime les **œufs** bouillis au petit déujeuner.

Jhairm layzeur boowee oh petee dayjheurnay.

I like boiled eggs for breakfast.

Où est la **laisse** du chien? C'est l'heure de la promenade.

Oo ay la less dew sheeang? Say leur duh la promenad.

Where's the dog's lead lead? It's time for his walk.

Maman boit deux **tasses** de thé avant le travail.

Mammon bwa duh tass duh tay avvon luh trav-eye.

Mum drinks two cups of tea before work.

Tous les matins, je bois un verre de **jus d'orange**.

Too lay mattang, jhuh bwa un vair duh jhew doronjh.

Every morning, I drink a glass of orange juice.

Tous les élèves s'occupent
dans la salle de classe.

**Too layzaylairve sokyupe
don la sal duh classe.**

le bon point
luh bon pwang
gold star

les numéros
lay newmeroh
numbers

la règle
la rairgl
ruler

le globe terrestre
luh globe terrestr
globe

les stylos
lay steeloh
pens

l'ordinateur
lordinateur
computer

la souris
la sooree
mouse

le clavier
luh klaveeay
keyboard

la maîtresse
la mairtress
teacher

123456789
2+4=6
7-3=
abcdefghijk

La maîtresse se fâche si on regarde par la **fenêtre** quand elle parle.

La mairtress suh fash see on regard par luh fenairtr kontell parl.

The teacher gets cross if you look out of the window when she is talking.

Je ne peux pas tracer des traits droits sans **règle**.

Jhuh nuh puh pa trassay day tray drwa son rairgl.

I can't draw straight lines without a ruler.

Où sont les **stylos**? J'ai besoin de m'entraîner à écrire.

Oo son lay steeloh? Jhay beswang duh montrairnay a aycreer.

Where are the pens? I need to practise my writing.

Je peux taper sur le **clavier** sans regarder.

Jhuh puh tappay syur luh klaveeay son regarday.

I can type on the keyboard without looking.

Le poisson rouge vit dans un **aquarium**.

Luh pwasson roojh vee donzun akwahrium.

The goldfish lives in a fish tank.

Peux-tu me prêter ton **crayon** rouge?

Puh tew muh prettay ton krayong roojh?

Can you lend me your red pencil?

J'ai fait un très beau **dessin** d'un poisson.
Jhay fay un tray boh dessang dun pwasson.
I have done a brilliant drawing of a fish.

L'**horloge** affiche onze heures et demie – c'est pas longtemps avant le déjeuner.
Lorlojh affeesh onzeur ay demee – say pa longtom avvon luh dayjheurnay.
The clock says half past eleven – not long until lunchtime.

Regardez la France sur le **globe terrestre**.
Regarday la Fronce syur luh globe terrestr.
Look at France on the globe.

Peux-tu fermer la **porte**? C'est froid!
Puh tew fairmay la port? Say fwa!
Can you close the door? It's cold!

La **maîtresse** me dit que mon cahier n'est pas très propre.
La mairtress muh dee kuh mon kahyay nay pa tray propr.
The teacher tells me that my notebook is not very neat.

Tout le monde aime recevoir un **bon point**.
Too luh mond airm ressevwar un bon pwang.
Everyone likes getting a gold star.

Les enfants accompagnent
Maman au supermarché.

**Layzonfon accompanyer
Mammon oh supermarshay.**

la banane
la banan
banana

les biscuits
lay biskwee
biscuits

le gâteau
luh gattoh
cake

la sucette
la sussett
lollipop

les haricot
lay aricoh
(tinned) beans

le fromage
luh fromarjh
cheese

la carotte
la carott
carrot

la tomate
la tomatt
tomato

Je suis tombé sur
un os – je n'ai pas
d'argent!

le magazine
luh magazine
magazine

le journal
luh jhoornal
newspaper

14

le lave-vaisselle
luh lav-vayssell
washing-up liquid

le promotion
luh promosyon
special offer

la nourriture pour chiens
la noorityur poor sheeang
(tinned) dog food

le jambon
luh jhombon
ham

le vélo
luh vayloh
bicycle

la caisse
la kess
(checkout) till

l'argent
larjhon
money

le caddie
luh kaddy
trolley

15

Les **sucettes** ne sont pas bons pour les dents!

Lay sussett nuh son pa bon poor lay don!

Lollipops are not good for the teeth!

Peux-tu acheter ce **magazine** pour moi?

Puh tew ashtay suh magazine poor mwa?

Can you buy this magazine for me?

La **caddie** a une roue qui grince – on dirait une souris!

La kaddy a une roo key grance – on deeray une sooree!

The trolley has a squeaky wheel – it sounds like a mouse!

Il y a des affiches de **promotion** partout dans le supermarché.

Eelya dayzaffeesh duh promosyon partoo don luh supermarshay.

There are special-offer signs all over the supermarket.

Ne laisse pas le chien voler le **jambon**!

Nuh less pa luh sheeang vollay luh jhombon!

Don't let the dog steal the ham!

N'oubliez pas la **nourriture pour chien** – le chien a faim.

Noobleeay pa la noorityur poor sheeang – luh sheeang a fang.

Don't forget the dog food – the dog is hungry.

J'ai laissé mon **vélo** dehors. J'espère qu'il ne pleuvra pas!

Jhay lessay mon vayloh duh-oar. Jhespair keel nuh pleuvra pa!

I've left my bicycle outside. I hope it doesn't rain!

Maman dit que nous ne pouvons pas acheter des **biscuits**.

Mammon dee kuh noo nuh poovon pazashtay day biskwee.

Mum says we can't buy any biscuits.

Maman a amené des **gâteaux** à son travail pour son anniversaire.

Mammon a amenay day gattoh a son trav-eye poor son anivairsair.

Mum took some cakes to work on her birthday.

J'ai dépensé tout mon **argent** pour les bonbons.

Jhai dayponsay too monarjhon poor lay bonbon.

I have spent all my money on sweets.

Nous n'avons pas besoin de **tomates**.

Noo navonpa beswang duh tomatt.

We don't need any tomatoes.

Achetons du **fromage** pour faire des sandwiches.

Ashtong dew fromarjh poor fair day sondweech.

Let's buy some cheese to make sandwiches.

Ils prennent Napoléon au parc
pour aller pour un pique-nique.

**Eel pren Napolayon oh park
poor allay poor un peekneek.**

la balançoire
la balonswar
swing

le toboggan
luh tobogong
slide

le tape-cul
luh tap-cewl
seesaw

l'étang
laytong
pond

le casque
luh kask
helmet

les pommes
lay pom
apples

la limonade
la limonad
lemonade

les chips
lay sheeps
crisps

le skateboard
luh skateboard
skateboard

la boue
la boo
mud

le pain
luh pang
bread

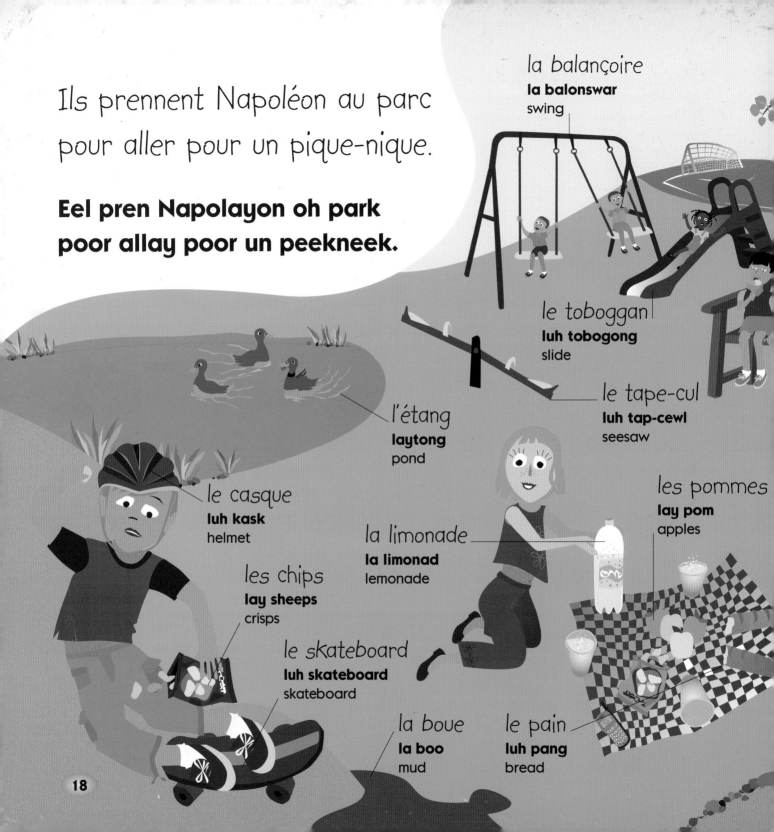

18

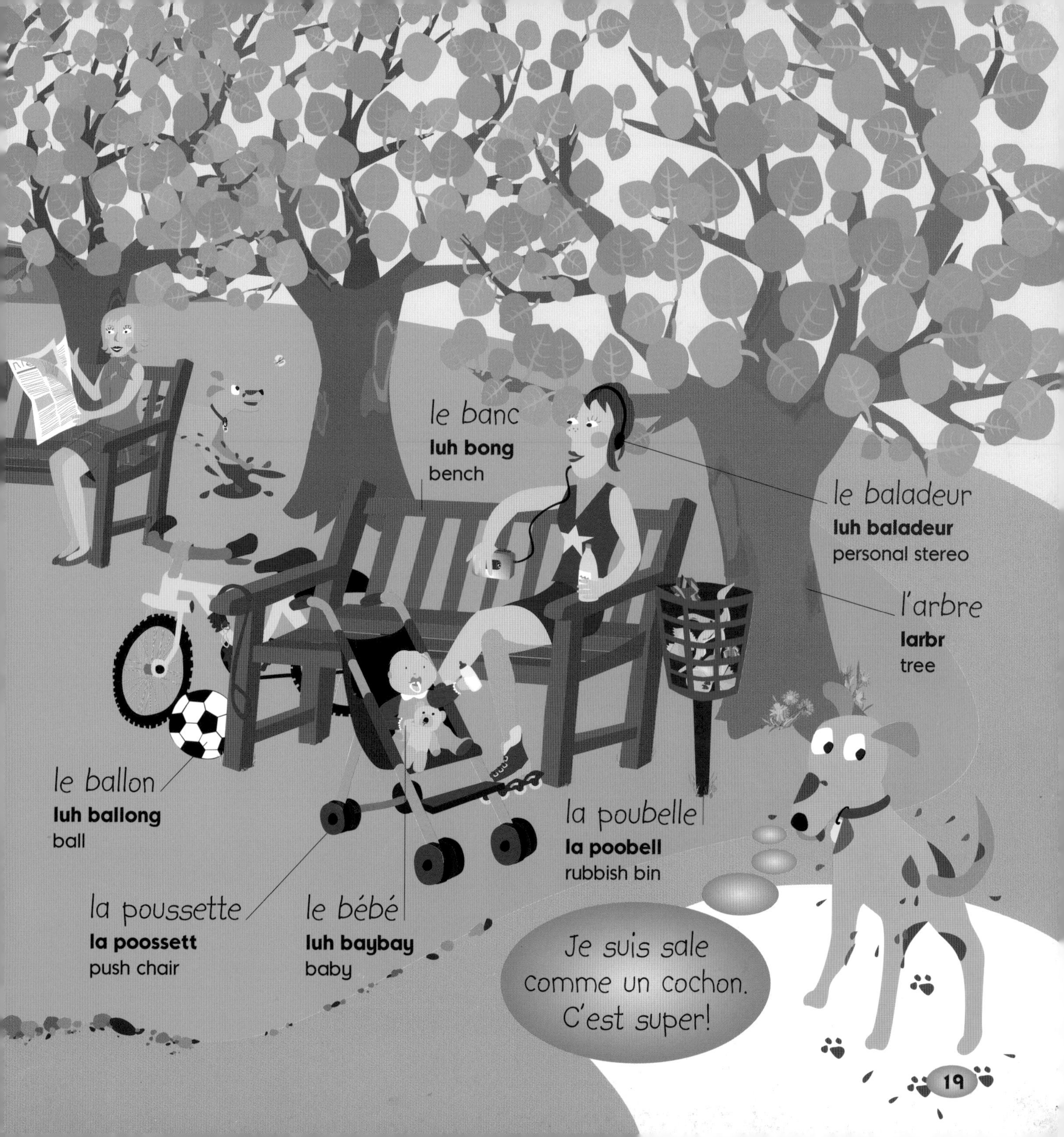

le banc
luh bong
bench

le baladeur
luh baladeur
personal stereo

l'arbre
larbr
tree

le ballon
luh ballong
ball

la poubelle
la poobell
rubbish bin

la poussette
la poossett
push chair

le bébé
luh baybay
baby

Je suis sale comme un cochon. C'est super!

19

Les **arbres** sont super pour jouer à cache-cache.
Lays arbr son supair poor jhooay a cashcash.
The trees are great for playing hide-and-seek.

Peux-tu me pousser sur la **balançoire**?
Puh tew muh poossay syur la balonswar?
Can you push me on the swing?

J'ai faim. Est-ce que je peux manger du **pain** et du fromage?
Jhay fang. Esker jhuh puh monjhay dew pang ay dew fromarjh?
I'm hungry. Can I have some bread and cheese?

Où est Maman? Elle se repose sur le **banc**.
Oo ay Mammon? Ell suh repose syur luh bong.
Where's Mum? She's having a rest on the bench.

Miam, les **pommes** sont délicieuses, toutes croquantes, douces et juteuses.
Miam, lay pom son daylisyerz, toot crokont, dooce ay jhewterz.
Mmmm, the apples are delicious, all crunchy, sweet and juicy.

J'aime jouer avec le **ballon**, surtout quand je marque un but.
Jhairm jhooay avek luh ballong, syurtoo kon jhuh mark un bew.
I like playing with the ball, especially when I score a goal.

Qu'est-ce qu'on boit au pique-nique?
De la **limonade**, bien sûr.
Keskon bwa oh peekneek? Dela limonad, beeang syur.
What are we drinking at the picnic? Lemonade, of course.

Ça fait mal quand je tombe de
mon **skateboard**.
Sa fay mal kon jhuh tombe duh mon skateboard.
It hurts when I fall off my skateboard.

Ramasse ces ordures et mets-les á la **poubelle**!
Ramass sayzordyur ay may lay a la poobell!
Pick up that rubbish and put it in the bin!

Mon chien aime jouer dans la **boue** – il pense
que c'est drôle!
Mon sheeang airm jhooay don la boo – eel ponce kuh say droll!
My dog likes playing in the mud – he thinks it's fun!

Ne mange pas la glace sur le **tape-cul**!
Nuh monjh pa la glasse syur luh tap-cewl!
Don't eat ice cream on the seesaw!

Manger les **chips** en jouant – c'est fou!
Monjhay lay sheeps on jhouon – say foo!
Eating crisps while playing – that's crazy!

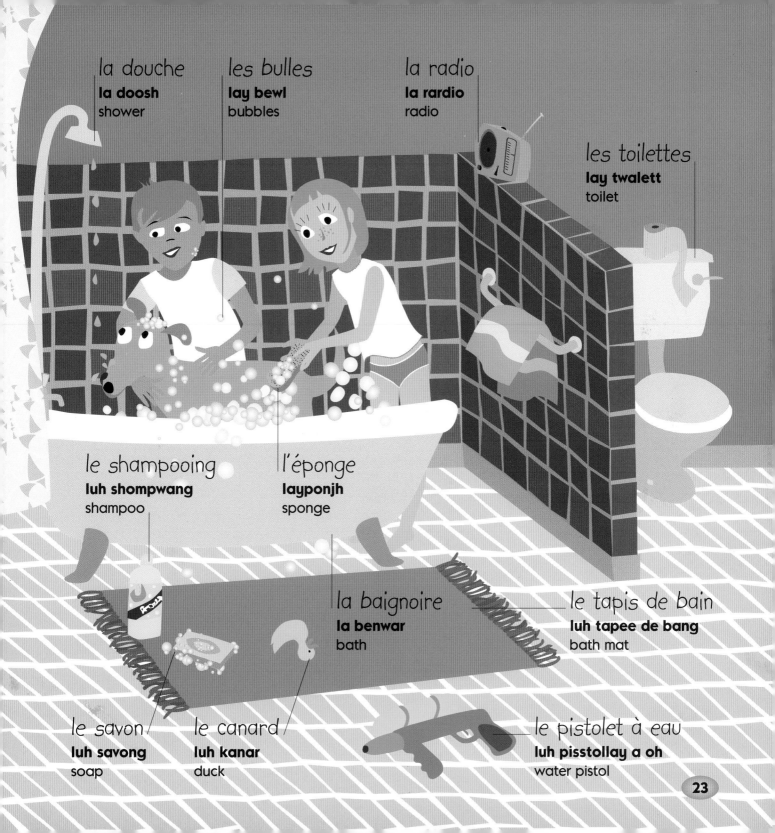

la douche
la doosh
shower

les bulles
lay bewl
bubbles

la radio
la rardio
radio

les toilettes
lay twalett
toilet

le shampooing
luh shompwang
shampoo

l'éponge
layponjh
sponge

la baignoire
la benwar
bath

le tapis de bain
luh tapee de bang
bath mat

le savon
luh savong
soap

le canard
luh kanar
duck

le pistolet à eau
luh pisstollay a oh
water pistol

23

Maman m'a dit de me laver les mains dans le **lavabo**.

Mammon maddee duh muh lavvay lay mang don luh lavaboh.

Mum told me to wash my hands in the basin.

La bouteille de **shampooing** est presque vide.

La bootay duh shompwang ay presk veed.

The bottle of shampoo is nearly empty.

Le **tapis de bain** est tout trempé! Qui a éclaboussé?

Luh tapee duh bang ay too trompay! Key a ayclaboossay?

The bath mat is all wet! Who's been splashing?

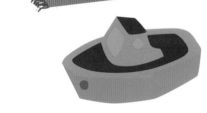

On jouait avec le **bâteau** dans le bain comme bébé.

On jhooay avek luh batoh don luh bang com baybay.

We used to play with the boat in the bath as babies.

Le chien l'aime quand on lui enlève son **collier**.

Luh sheeang lairm konton lwee onlairv son kollyay.

The dog likes it when we take off his collar.

Écoute! Il y a ta chanson préférée à la **radio**.

Aycoot! Eelya ta shonson prayfayray a la rardio.

Listen! Your favourite song is on the radio.

Ne laissez pas le chien jouer avec le **canard**!
Nuh lessay pa luh sheeang jhooay avek luh kanar!
Don't let the dog play with the duck!

J'ai perdu ma **brosse à dents**.
Jhay pairdew ma brossadong.
I've lost my toothbrush.

J'est bon de se sècher avec une **serviette** douce.

C'est bon de se sècher avec une **serviette** douce.
Say bon duh suh seshay avek une sairvyett dooce.
It's good to dry yourself with a soft towel.

Papa nous a grondés quand nous avons fait du désordre avec le **pistolet à eau**.
Pappa nooza gronday kon noozavon fay dew dayzordr avek luh pisstollay a oh.
Dad told us off when we made a mess with the water pistol.

J'aime les bains avec beaucoup de **bulles**.
Jhairm lay bang avek boh-coo duh bewl.
I like baths with lots of bubbles.

Papa dit qu'il faut se dépêcher. Il veut utiliser les **toilettes**!
Pappa dee keel foh suh daypeshay. Eel vuh yewtileezay lay twalett!
Dad says we have to hurry up. He wants to use the toilet!

Il faut se coucher. Les enfants et Napoléon sont tous fatigués.

Eel foh suh cooshay. Layzonfon ay Napolayon son toos fateegay.

l'étoile
laytwal
star

le poster
luh postair
poster

la casquette
la kaskett
cap

les bandes dessinées
lay bond desseenay
comics

la lampe
la lomp
lamp

Quelle journée! Je suis tout á fait crevé.

la chaussette
la shohssett
sock

les baskets
lay baskett
trainers

le réveil
luh rayvay
alarm clock

la poupée
la poopay
doll

les perles
lay pairl
beads

le journal intime
luh jhoornal anteem
diary

le nounours
luh noonoors
teddy bear

le livre
luh leevr
book

le verre d'eau
luh vair doh
glass of water

le lit
luh lee
bed

les pantoufles
lay pontoofler
slippers

la couette
la koowett
duvet

la chemise de nuit
la shermeez duh nwee
nightshirt

la brosse à cheveux
la brossa-sher-vuh
hairbrush

J'aime afficher les **posters** des artistes pop dans ma chambre.

Jhairm affeeshay lay postair dayzarteest pop don ma shombr.
I like putting up posters of pop stars in my bedroom.

Mon **livre** favori est si marrant. Cela me fait éclater de rire!

Mon leevr favoree ay see marron. Sela muh fay ayclatay duh rear!
My favourite book is so funny. It makes me laugh out loud!

C'est utile d'avoir un **verre** d'eau près du lit.

Settewteel davwar un vair doh pray dew lee.
It's useful to have a glass of water by the bed.

Je porterais mes **baskets** tout le temps si je pouvais.

Jhuh porteray may baskett too luh tom see jhuh poovay.
I'd wear my trainers all the time if I could.

Chaque nuit, je m'endors en câlinant mon **nounours**.

Shak nwee, jhuh mondoor on kaleenon mon noonoors.
Every night, I go to sleep cuddling my teddy bear.

On peut écrire des secrets dans un **journal intime**.

On puh aycreer day secray donzun jhoornal anteem.
You can write secrets in a diary.

Ces **chaussettes** sentent vraiment mauvais!
Say shohssett sont vraymon mohvay!
These socks smell really bad!

Mon chat aime se coucher sur mon **lit**.
Mon sha airm suh kooshay syur mon lee.
My cat likes sleeping on my bed.

Je dois mettre mon **réveil** – je vais à
l'école demain.
Jhuh dwa mettr mon rayvay – jhuh vay alaycoll demang.
I must set my alarm clock – it's school tomorrow.

On lit souvent les **bandes dessinées** tard
dans la nuit.
On lee soovon lay bond desseenay tar don la nwee.
We often read comics late at night.

Tu as vu ma **brosse à cheveux**? J'ai les cheveux
très mélés.
Tew a view ma brossa-sher-vuh? Jhay lay sher-vuh tray maylay.
Have you seen my hairbrush? My hair is really tangled.

Mes **pantoufles** gardent mes pieds au chaud.
May pontoofler gard may peeay oh shoh.
My slippers keep my toes cosy.

Index

Is there a particular word you'd like to learn in French? This index features all the key words found in the book (in English followed by the French translation) as well as lots of other useful and interesting words selected from the sentences and Napoléon's thoughts.

KL

keyboard – **le clavier** 10, 12
kind – **gentil/gentille** 8
knife – **le couteau** 7, 8
lamp – **la lampe** 26
lead – **la laisse** 6, 9
lemonade
  – **la limonad** 18, 21
(to) like – **aimer** 9, 13, 20, 21,
  24, 25, 28, 29
lollipop – **la sucette** 14, 16
lunch – **le déjeuner** 6, 8

MNO

magazine
  – **le magazine** 14, 16
milk – **le lait** 6, 8
money – **l'argent** 14, 15, 17, 32
morning – **le matin** 9
mouse – **la souris** 10, 16
mud – **la boue** 18, 21
Mum – **Maman** 7, 8, 9, 14, 16,
  17, 20, 24
newspaper – **le journal** 14
night – **la nuit** 28, 29
nightshirt
  – **la chemise de nuit** 27
number – **le numéro** 10
orange juice – **le jus d'orange**
  7, 9

PR

pants – **le caleçon** 22
park – **le parc** 18
pencil – **le crayon** 11, 12
pen – **le stylo** 10, 12
personal stereo
  – **le baladeur** 19
picnic – **le pique-nique** 18, 21
pig – **le cochon** 19, 32
plate – **l'assiette** 22, 32

(to) play – **jouer** 20, 21, 24, 25
pond – **l'étang** 18
pop star – **l'artiste pop** 28
poster – **le poster** 26, 28
pupil – **l'élève** 10
push chair – **la poussette** 19
radio – **la radio** 23, 24
rain – **la pluie** 17
red – **rouge** 12
room – **la chambre** 28
rubbish bin
  – **la poubelle** 19, 21
rucksack – **le sac à dos** 11
ruler – **la règle** 10, 12

S

sandwich – **le sandwich** 17
school – **l'école** 8, 29
seesaw – **le tape-cul** 18,21
shampoo
  – **le shampooing** 23, 24
shower – **la douche** 23
skateboard
  – **le skateboard** 18, 21
slide – **le toboggan** 18
slippers – **les pantoufles** 27, 29
(to) smell – **sentir** 29
soap – **le savon** 23
sock – **la chausette** 26, 29
song – **la chanson** 24
special offer
  – **le promotion** 15, 16
sponge – **l'éponge** 23
spoon – **la cuillère** 7
star – **l'étoile** 26
(to) steal – **voler** 16
strawberry – **la fraise** 8
supermarket
  – **le supermarché** 14, 16
sweet – **le bonbon** 17
swing – **la balançoire** 18, 20

T

table – **la table** 11
(to) talk – **parler** 12
tap – **le robinet** 22
(to) taste – **goûter** 8
tea – **le thé** 9
teacher – **la maîtresse/le maître**
  10, 12, 13
teacher's pet – **le chouchou**
  du prof 11, 32
teddy bear – **le nounours** 27,
  28
(to) think – **penser** 21
tired – **fatigué** 26
toilet – **les toilettes** 23, 25
tomato – **la tomate** 14, 17
tomorrow – **demain** 29
tooth – **la dent** 4, 16
toothbrush
  – **la brosse à dents** 22, 25
towel – **la serviette** 22, 25
trainers – **les baskets** 26, 28
tree – **l'arbre** 19, 20
trolley – **le caddie** 15, 16

UW

(to) use – **utiliser** 25
(to) walk – **se promener** 9
(to) wash – **laver** 24
washing-up lquid
  – **le lave-vaiselle** 15
water – **l'eau** 27, 28
water pistol
  – **le pistolet à eau** 23, 25
(to) wear – **porter** 28
(to) wet – **tremper** 24
wheel – **la roue** 16
window – **la fenêtre** 11, 12
wolf – **le loup** 6, 32
(to) work – **travailler** 8, 11
(to) write – **écrire** 28

Napoléon's thoughts!

p.6 *Où est mon petit déjeuner? J'ai faim de loup!*
Oo ay mon petee dayjeurnay? Jhay fam duh loo!
Where's my breakfast? I'm as hungry as a wolf!
(I'm starving.)

p.11 *Je suis le chouchou du prof.*
Jhuh swee luh shooshoo dew prof.
I'm the teacher's little cabbage.
(I'm the teacher's pet.)

p.14 *Je suis tombé sur un os –*
je n'ai pas d'argent!
Jhuh swee tombay syur un ohs – jhuh nay pa darjhon!
I've fallen on a bone (I've got a problem) –
I haven't got any money.

p.19 *Je suis sale comme un cochon. C'est super!*
Jhuh swee sarl com un koshong. Say supair!
I'm dirty like a pig. (I'm filthy.) It's great!

p.22 *Je ne suis pas dans mon assiette –*
je déteste prendre un bain!
**Jhuh nuh swee pa don mon asseeyet – jhuh daytest
prondr un bang!**
I'm not in my plate (I'm not myself) –
I hate having a bath!

p.26 *Quelle journée! Je suis tout á fait crevé.*
Kel jhoornay! Jhuh swee toot a fay krevay.
What a day! I'm completely ready to burst. (I'm exhausted.)